Works in English by Czeslaw Milosz

The Captive Mind

Postwar Polish Poetry: An Anthology

Native Realm: A Search for Self-Definition

Selected Poems by Zbigniew Herbert
(translated by Czeslaw Milosz and Peter Dale Scott)

The History of Polish Literature

Selected Poems

Mediterranean Poems by Aleksander Wat
(translated by Czeslaw Milosz)

Emperor of the Earth: Modes of Eccentric Vision

Bells in Winter

The Witness of Poetry

The Issa Valley

Seizure of Power

Visions from San Francisco Bay

The Separate Notebooks

The Land of Ulro

Unattainable Earth

Unattainable Earth

CZESLAW MILOSZ

UNATTAINABLE
EARTH

Translated by the author

and Robert Hass

The Ecco Press

New York

Published by The Ecco Press in 1986
Published simultaneously in Canada by
Penguin Books Canada Ltd.
2801 John Street
Markham, Ontario, Canada L3R 1 B4
Printed in the United States of America
Library of Congress Cataloging in Publication Data
Milosz, Czeslaw.
Unattainable earth.
I. Hass, Robert. II. Title.
PG7158.M553A25 1986   891.8′58709   85-20617
ISBN 0-88001-098-3
ISBN 0-88001-102-5 (ppbk.)

Grateful acknowledgment is made to the following publications in which
these poems first appeared: The New Yorker: "After Paradise," "Anka,"
"At Noon," "Elegy for Y.Z.," "My-ness," "Return to Cracow in 1880,"
"Rustling Taffetas," "Table I," "Table II," "Winter." The New
York Review of Books: "Father Ch., Many Years Later," "Prepara-
tion," The Threepenny Review: "1913." Antaeus:
"Into the Tree," "On Prayer," "Consciousness," "Poet at Seventy."

Contents

Part Two
Unexpressed

Part Three
Unattainable Earth

Part Four
Consciousness

Part Five
I, He, She

Part Six
A Table

Preface

It is customary among poets to gather poems written during a few years and to compose them into a volume provided with a title. That custom, upon reflection, persists by dint of inherited habits, but has nothing self-evident in it. For a given servant of the Muses was in that period not only busy creating ideal objects that bear the name of poems. He lived among people, was feeling, thinking, getting acquainted with others' thoughts, and tried to capture the surrounding world by any means, including the act of the poem, but not only. In everything he wrote then the same striving and the same tone could be discerned, as we move in our life through successive renewals and incarnations, each of which has its own tone. Why then separate what is unified in time, in my case by the years 1981–1984? Why not include in one book, along with my own poems, poems by others, notes in prose, quotations from various sources and even fragments of letters from friends if all these pieces serve one purpose: my attempt to approach the inexpressible sense of being? Such a design I adopted in this book, searching, as I have once said, for "a more spacious form." And I hope that under the surface of somewhat odd multiformity, the reader will recognize a deeper unity.

The composition of this book follows that of the original volume published under the title *Nieobjeta ziemia,* which means roughly "earth too huge to be grasped." It includes several poems by Walt Whitman and D. H. Lawrence, in my translation into Polish. Robert Hass was of the opinion that those poems should not be eliminated, as they make an integral part of my mosaic, so we have left them, an homage to tutelary spirits.

—C.M.

Our life consists partly in folly, partly in good sense; whoever writes on it only in a staid fashion and with measure, leaves more than half of himself behind.

—MONTAIGNE, *Essays*

Let man be noble,
Kind to his neighbors, good!
For only then is he different
From all the creatures we know.

Glory to Higher Spirits!
Unknown, guessed only!
Let man's example teach us
That we can put faith in them.

—GOETHE

Part One

The Garden of
Earthly Delights

The Garden of Earthly Delights

1/Summer

In the July sun they were leading me to the Prado,
Straight to the room where *The Garden of Earthly Delights*
Had been prepared for me. So that I run to its waters
And immerse myself in them and recognize myself.

The twentieth century is drawing to its close.
I will be immured in it like a fly in amber.
I was old but my nostrils craved new scents
And through my five senses I received a share in the earth
Of those who led me, our sisters and lovers.

How lightly they walk! Their hips in trousers, not in trailing
    dresses,
Their feet in sandals, not on cothurni,
Their hair not clasped by a tortoiseshell buckle.
Yet constantly the same, renewed by the moon, Luna,
In a chorus that keeps praising Lady Venus.

Their hands touched my hands and they marched, gracious,
As if in the early morning at the outset of the world.

[3

2/A Ball

It is going on inside a transparent ball
Above which God the Father, short, with a trimmed beard,
Sits with a book, enveloped in dark clouds.
He reads an incantation and things are called to being.
As soon as the earth emerges, it bears grasses and trees.
We are those to whom green hills have been offered
And for us this ray descends from opened mists.
Whose hand carries the ball? Probably the Son's.
And the whole Earth is in it, Paradise and Hell.

3/Paradise

Under my sign, Cancer, a pink fountain
Pours out four streams, the sources of four rivers.
But I don't trust it. As I verified myself,
That sign is not lucky. Besides we abhor
The moving jaws of crabs and the calcareous
Cemeteries of the ocean. This, then, is the Fountain
Of Life? Toothed, sharp-edged,
With its innocent, delusive color. And beneath,
Just where the birds alight, glass traps set with glue.
A white elephant, a white giraffe, white unicorns,
Black creatures of the ponds. A lion mauls a deer.
A cat has a mouse. A three-headed lizard,
A three-headed ibis, their meaning unknown.
Or a two-legged dog, no doubt a bad omen.
Adam sits astonished. His feet
Touch the foot of Christ who has brought Eve
And keeps her right hand in his left while lifting
Two fingers of his right like the one who teaches.
Who is she, and who will she be, the beloved
From the Song of Songs? This Wisdom-Sophia,
Seducer, the Mother and Ecclesia?
Thus he created her who will conceive him?
Where then did he get his human form
Before the years and centuries began?
Human, did he exist before the beginning?
And establish a Paradise, though incomplete,
So that she might pluck the fruit, she, the mysterious one,
Whom Adam contemplates, not comprehending?

[5

I am these two, twofold. I ate from the tree
Of knowledge. I was expelled by the archangel's sword.
At night I sensed her pulse. Her mortality.
And we have searched for the real place ever since.

4/Earth

Riding birds, feeling under our thighs the soft feathers
Of goldfinches, orioles, kingfishers,
Or spurring lions into a run, unicorns, leopards,
Whose coats brush against our nakedness,
We circle the vivid and abundant waters,
Mirrors from which emerge a man's and a woman's head,
Or an arm, or the round breasts of the sirens.
Every day is the day of berry harvest here.
The two of us bite into wild strawberries
Bigger than a man, we plunge into cherries,
We are drenched with the juices of their wine,
We celebrate the colors of carmine
And vermillion, as in toys on a Christmas tree.
We are many, a whole tribe swarming,
And so like each other that our lovemaking
Is as sweet and immodest as a game of hide-and-seek.
And we lock ourselves inside the crowns of flowers
Or in transparent, iridescent bubbles.
Meanwhile a flock of lunar signs fills the sky
To prepare the alchemical nuptials of the planets.

5/Earth Again

They are incomprehensible, the things of this earth.
The lure of waters. The lure of fruits.
Lure of the two breasts and long hair of a maiden.
In rouge, in vermillion, in that color of ponds
Found only in the Green Lakes near Wilno.
And ungraspable multitudes swarm, come together
In the crinkles of tree bark, in the telescope's eye,
For an endless wedding,
For the kindling of the eyes, for a sweet dance
In the elements of the air, sea, earth and subterranean caves,
So that for a short moment there is no death
And time does not unreel like a skein of yarn
Thrown into an abyss.

After Paradise

Don't run any more. Quiet. How softly it rains
On the roofs of the city. How perfect
All things are. Now, for the two of you
Waking up in a royal bed by a garret window.
For a man and a woman. For one plant divided
Into masculine and feminine which longed for each other.
Yes, this is my gift to you. Above ashes
On a bitter, bitter earth. Above the subterranean
Echo of clamorings and vows. So that now at dawn
You must be attentive: the tilt of a head,
A hand with a comb, two faces in a mirror
Are only forever once, even if unremembered,
So that you watch what is, though it fades away,
And are grateful every moment for your being.
Let that little park with greenish marble busts
In the pearl-gray light, under a summer drizzle,
Remain as it was when you opened the gate.
And the street of tall peeling porticos
Which this love of yours suddenly transformed.

The Hooks of a Corset

In a big city, on the boulevards, early. The raising of jalousies and marquees, sprinkled slabs of sidewalk, echo of steps, the spotted bark of trees. My twentieth century was beginning and they walked, men and women; it is now close to its end and they walk, not exactly the same but pattering the same way with shoes and high-heeled slippers. The impenetrable order of a division into the male and female sex, into old and young, without decrease, always here, instead of those who once lived. And I, breathing the air, enchanted because I am one of them, identifying my flesh with their flesh, but at the same time aware of beings who might not have perished. I, replacing them, bearing a different name yet their own because the five senses are ours in common, I am walking here, now, before I am replaced in my turn. We are untouched by death and time, children, myself with Eve, in a kindergarten, in a sandbox, in a bed, embracing each other, making love, saying the words of eternal avowals and eternal delights. The space wide open, glittering machines up above, the rumble of the metro below. And our dresses under heaven, tinfoil crowns, tights, imitation animal hair, the scales of lizard-birds. To absorb with your eyes the inside of a flower shop, to hear the voices of people, to feel on your tongue the taste of just-drunk coffee. Passing by the windows of apartments, I invent stories, similar to my own, a lifted elbow, the combing of hair before a mirror. I multiplied myself and came to inhabit every one of them separately, thus my impermanence has no power over me.

.   .   .

"And he sets off! and he watches the river of vitality flowing, so majestic and so brilliant. He admires the eternal beauty and astonishing harmony of life in the capitals, harmony so providentially maintained in the turmoil of human freedom. He contemplates the landscapes of big cities, landscapes caressed by mists or struck by the sun. He delights in beautiful carriages, proud horses, the spic-and-span cleanliness of grooms, the dexterity of footmen, the beauty of undulating women, in pretty children happy to be alive and well-dressed; to put it briefly, in universal life. If a fashion, the cut of dresses changes slightly, if knotted ribbons or buckles are dethroned by a cockade, if the bonnet grows larger and the chignon descends to the nape of the neck, if the waistline goes up and the skirt is simplified, do not doubt that his eagle's eye even at a great distance will take notice. A regiment is passing, perhaps on its way to the end of the world, throwing into the air its enticing flourish, light as hope: and already Mr. G. saw, examined, analyzed the arms, the gait, and the physiognomy of that unit. Shoulder-belts, sparklings, music, resolute looks, heavy and ponderous moustaches, all that penetrates him pell-mell; and in a few minutes a poem which results from it will be composed. And already his soul lives with the life of that regiment which is marching as one animal, a proud image of joy in obedience!

But evening comes. It is the bizarre and ambiguous hour when the curtains of the sky are drawn, when the cities light up. The gas makes a spot on the crimson of the sunset. Honest or dishonest, reasonable or crazy, people say to themselves: 'At last the day is over!' Wise men and rascals think of pleasure and everybody runs to a chosen place to drink the cup of oblivion. Mr. G. will remain to the last wherever the light still glows,

poetry resounds, life teems, music vibrates; wherever a passion
can pose for his eye, wherever the natural man and the man of
convention show themselves in a strange beauty, wherever the
sun witnesses the hurried pleasures of a *depraved animal.*"

—CHARLES BAUDELAIRE,
"Constantin Guys, painter of modern life"

.　　.　　.

I am engaged in a serious operation, devoted to it exclusively, and for that reason I am released from the reproach of shirking my social duties. In the Quartier Latin, when bells ring for the New Year 1900, I am the one who walks uphill on rue Cujas. A gloved hand is linked to my arm and the gas hisses in the street lamps. Her flesh which has turned to dust is as desirable to me as it was to that other man and if I touch her in my dream she does not even mention that she has died long ago. On the verge of a great discovery I almost penetrate the secret of the Particular transforming itself into the General and of the General transforming itself into the Particular. I endow with a philosophical meaning the moment when I helped her to undo the hooks of her corset.

. . .

INSCRIPT

"She was fond of tailored dresses from Vienna, very modest but rustling with linings made of iridescent taffeta; she would carry a rarely used lorgnon on a long chain interspersed with tiny pearls, and a bracelet with pendants. Her movements were slow and somewhat affected, she offered her hand to be kissed with a studied gesture, probably under her calm she was concealing the timidity characteristic of her whole family. Her jewelry, cigarette case, and perfume bore the stamp of an individual and fastidious taste. Her literary preferences were rather revolutionary and progressive. Much more vividly and sincerely than did Lela, she took an interest in her reading but in fact books were for her accessories to her dress, like a hat or an umbrella. Aunt Isia was the first to introduce Doroszewicze to the fashionable Tetmajer, then she brought the photographs of Ghirlandaio's and Botticelli's paintings from Italy and talked about the school of the early Renaissance, finally she took a liking to Przybyszewski and his style, and would often say: 'Do you want white peacocks?—I will give you white peacocks. Do you want crimson amethysts?—I will give you crimson amethysts.' "

—JANINA ŻÓTTOWSKA,
Inne czasy, Inni ludzie (Other Times, Other People)

•   •   •

[14

Rustling taffetas. At sunset in a park by the Prypet River.
The party sets out for a walk on a path lined with flowers.
The fragrance of nicotianas, phlox and resedas.
Great silence, the empty expanse of rising waters.
Meanwhile the servants bring in lamps, set the table for supper.
And the dining room windows lit the agaves on the lawn.

Lela, Marishka, Sophineta! Lenia, Stenia, Isia, Lilka!
Is it fair that I will never talk with you
In a language not disguised by etiquette
As less than language and not reduced to table chatter
But austere and precise like a thought
That attempts to embrace the poor lives of beings?

I walk about. No longer human. In a hunting outfit.
Visiting our thick forests and the houses and manors.
Cold borscht is served and I am abstracted
With disturbing questions from the end of my century,
Mainly regarding the truth, where does it come from, where is
    it?
Mum, I was eating chicken with cucumber salad.

My pretty ones, abducted, beyond will and guilt.
My awareness harrows me as well as my silence.
All my life I gathered up images and ideas,
I learned how to travel through lost territories,
But the moment between birth and disappearance
Is too much, I know, for the meager word.

[15

Strings of wild ducks fly over the Respublica's waters.
Dew falls on Polish manners imported from Warsaw and Vienna.
I cross the river in a dugout to the village side.
Barking dogs greet me there and the bell of an Orthodox church.

What would I like to tell you? That I didn't get what I looked
      for:
To gather all of us naked on the earthly pastures
Under the endless light of suspended time
Without that form which confines me as it once confined you.

Seeing the future. A diviner. In a soft merciful night.
When pigweed grows on the paths of a cut-down garden
And a narrow gold chain on a white neck,
Together with the memory of all of you, perishes.

. . .

[16

"In the Ukraine several hundred gardens of various sizes survived the fall of the Respublica and of the gentry whose presence was marked everywhere by old trees, lawns and decorative
shrubbery. Once, in the Eastern Carpathians, in a remote valley
distant by a whole day's walk from the nearest settlement, I
noticed, lost among hazels, one of those decorative shrubs characteristic of gardens from the beginning of the last century.
Parting raspberries and vines I found a few old stones and bricks.
Even in that wilderness the settlers had remained faithful to the
horticultural passion of the old Respublica."

—PAWEŁ HOSTOWIEC,
W dolinie Dniestru (In the Valley of the Dniester)

.   .   .

What did I really want to tell them? That I labored to transcend my place and time, searching for the Real. And here is my work done (commendably?), my life fulfilled, as it was destined to be, in grief. Now I appear to myself as one who was under the delusion of being his own while he was the subject of a style. Just as they were, so what if it was a different subjection. "Do you want white peacocks?—I will give you white peacocks." And we could have been united only by what we have in common: the same nakedness in a garden beyond time, but the moments are short when it seems to me that, at odds with time, we hold each other's hands. And I drink wine and I shake my head and say: "What man feels and thinks will never be expressed."

"If then you do not make yourself equal to God, you cannot apprehend God; for like is known by like. Leap clear of all that is corporeal, and make yourself grow to a like expanse with that greatness which is beyond measure; rise above all time, and become eternal; then you will apprehend God. Think that for you nothing is impossible; deem that you too are immortal, and that you are able to grasp all things in your thought, to know every craft and every science; find your home in the thoughts of every living creature; make yourself higher than all heights and lower than all depths; bring together in yourself all opposites of quality, heat and cold, dryness and fluidity; think that you are everywhere at once, on land, at sea, in heaven; think that you are not yet begotten, that you are in the womb, that you are young, that you are old, that you have died, that you are in the world beyond the grave; grasp in your thought all this at once, all times and places, all substances and qualities and magnitudes together; then you can apprehend God. But if you shut up your soul in your body, and abase yourself, and say, 'I know nothing, I can do nothing; I am afraid of earth and sky and sea, I cannot mount to heaven; I know not what I was or what I shall be'; then, what have you to do with God?"

—*Corpus Hermeticum*

INSCRIPT

"There is not and there cannot be anything more precious for any thinking creature than life. Death is an oddity tearing the spectator away from a huge stage before the play, which infinitely interests him, is over."

—CASANOVA, *Memoirs*

Annalena

It happened that sometimes I kissed in mirrors the reflection
of my face; since the hands, face and tears of Annalena had caressed
it, my face seemed to me divinely beautiful and as if suffused with
heavenly sweetness.

—O. MILOSZ, *L'Amoureuse initiation*

I liked your velvet yoni, Annalena, long voyages in the delta of
your legs.

A striving upstream toward your beating heart through more
and more savage currents saturated with the light of hops and
bindweed.

And our vehemence and triumphant laughter and our hasty
dressing in the middle of the night to walk on the stone stairs
of the upper city.

Our breath held by amazement and silence, porosity of worn-
out stones and the great door of the cathedral.

Over the gate of the rectory fragments of brick among weeds,
in darkness the touch of a rough buttressed wall.

And later our looking from the bridge down to the orchard,
when under the moon every tree is separate on its kneeler, and
from the secret interior of dimmed poplars the echo carries the
sound of a water turbine.

To whom do we tell what happened on the earth, for whom do
we place everywhere huge mirrors in the hope that they will be
filled up and will stay so?

[*21*

Always in doubt whether it was we who were there, you and I, Annalena, or just anonymous lovers on the enameled tablets of a fairyland.

Yellow Bicycle

When I ask her what she wants,
She says, "A yellow bicycle."
—ROBERT HASS

As long as we move at a dancing gait, my love,
Leaving the car by the place where a yellow bicycle stands, leaning
    against a tree,
As long as we enter the gardens at a dancing gait,
Northern gardens, full of dew and the voices of birds,
Our memory is childish and it saves only what we need:
Yesterday morning and evening, no further.
But then we recalled a girl who had a yellow bicycle like that
And used to talk to it in caressing words.
Later on, among flower beds between box hedges,
We saw a little statue and a plate with the sculptor's name.
We were descending by terraces toward a lake
Which is like a lake from an old ballad,
Smooth, between the peninsulas of spruce forests.
Thus common human memory visited us again.

Mystic

They call all experience of the senses *mystic,* when the experience is considered.
So an apple becomes *mystic* when I taste in it
the summer and the snows, the wild welter of earth
and the insistence of the sun.

All of which things I can surely taste in a good apple.
Though some apples taste preponderantly of water, wet and
sour,
and some of too much sun, brackish sweet
like lagoon-water that has been too much sunned.

If I say I taste these things in an apple, I am called *mystic,* which
means a liar.
The only way to eat an apple is to hog it down like a pig
and taste nothing
that is *real.*

But if I eat an apple, I like to eat it with all my senses awake.
Hogging it down like a pig I call the feeding of corpses.

—D. H. LAWRENCE

[*24*

The Man of Tyre

The man of Tyre went down to the sea
pondering, for he was Greek, that God is one and all alone and
    ever more shall be so.
And a woman who had been washing clothes in the pool of
    rock
where a stream came down to the gravel of the sea and sank in,
who had spread white washing on the gravel banked above the
    bay,
who had laid her shift on the shore, on the shingle slope,
who had waded to the pale green sea of evening, out to a shoal,
pouring sea-water over herself
now turned, and came slowly back, with her back to the eve-
    ning sky.

Oh lovely, lovely with the dark hair piled up, as she went deeper,
    deeper down the channel, then arose shallower, shallower,
with the full thighs slowly lifting of the wader wading shore-
    wards
and the shoulders pallid with light from the silent sky behind,
both breasts dim and mysterious, with the glamorous kindness
    of twilight between them
and the dim blotch of black maidenhair like an indicator,
giving a message to the man—

So in the canebrake he clasped his hands in delight
that could only be god-given, and murmured:
Lo! God is one god! But here in the twilight
godly and lovely comes Aphrodite out of the sea
towards me!

—D. H. LAWRENCE

[25

Pax

All that matters is to be at one with the living God
to be a creature in the house of the God of Life.

Like a cat asleep on a chair
at peace, in peace
and at one with the master of the house, with the mistress,
at home, at home in the house of the living,
sleeping on the hearth, and yawning before the fire.

Sleeping on the hearth of the living world
yawning at home before the fire of life
feeling the presence of the living God
like a great assurance
a deep calm in the heart
a presence
as of the master sitting at the board
in his own and greater being
in the house of life.

—D. H. LAWRENCE

Part Two

Unexpressed

To write a wise poem one must know more than what is expressed in it. Consciousness leaves every means of expression behind. Hence the regret that we will remain sillier in human memory than we were at the moments of our acutest comprehension.

A labyrinth. Constructed every day with words, with sounds of music, lines and colors of painting, masses of sculpture and architecture. Lasting for centuries, so absorbing the visitor that whoever plunges into it does not need the world anymore. A fortress, because it has been founded against the world. And the greatest wonder is this: if it becomes an object of delectation, it disintegrates like palaces woven of mist. For it is maintained only by a striving to go beyond it, somewhere, to the other unknown side.

INSCRIPT

"Rhythm is the highest expression of what we call thought, i.e., of the awareness and love of Movement."

—O. MILOSZ

INSCRIPT

"And perhaps art is for us liars the means of expressing the most imperative truths in a roundabout way?"

—O. MILOSZ

Into the Tree

The tree, says good Swedenborg, is a close relative of man.
Its boughs like arms join in an embrace.
The trees in truth are our parents,
We sprang from the oak, or perhaps, as the Greeks maintain,
    from the ash.

Our lips and tongue savor the fruit of the tree.
A woman's breast is called apple or pomegranate.
We love the womb as the tree loves the dark womb of the earth.
Thus, what is most desirable resides in a single tree,
And wisdom tries to touch its coarse-grained bark.

I learned, says the servant of the New Jerusalem,
That Adam in the garden, i.e., mankind's Golden Age,
Signifies the generations after the pre-adamites
Who are unjustly scorned though they were gentle,
Kind to each other, savage yet not bestial,
Happy in a land of fruits and springwaters.

Adam created in the image and in the likeness
Represents the parting of clouds covering the mind.

And Eve, why is she taken from Adam's rib?
—Because the rib is close to the heart, that's the name of self-
    love,
And Adam comes to know Eve, loving himself in her.

Above those two, the tree. A huge shade tree.

Of which the counselor of the Royal Mining Commission says
the following in his book *De amore conjugiali:*

"The Tree of Life signifies a man who lives from God, or God
living in man; and as love and wisdom, or charity and faith, or
good and truth, make the life of God in man, these are signified
by the Tree of Life, and hence the eternal life of the man. . . .
But the tree of science signifies the man who believes that he
lives from himself and not from God; thus that love and wisdom, or charity and faith, or good and truth, are in man from
himself and not from God; and he believes this because he thinks
and wills, and speaks and acts, in all likeness and appearance as
from himself."

Self-love offered the apple and the Golden Age was over.
After it, the Silver Age, the Bronze Age. And the Iron.

Then a child opens its eyes and sees a tree for the first time.
And people seem to us like walking trees.

[*31*

Since my youth I have tried to capture in words a reality such as I contemplated walking the streets of a human city and I have never succeeded; that is why each of my poems seems to me the token of an unaccomplished oeuvre. I learned early that language does not adhere to what we really are, that we move in a big make-believe which is maintained by books and pages of newsprint. And every one of my efforts to say something real ended the same way, by my being driven back to the enclosure of form, as if I were a sheep straying from the flock.

What will the poetry of the future be, which I think of but will never know? I know it is attainable because I experienced brief moments when it almost created itself under my pen, only to disappear immediately. The rhythm of the body will be in it, heartbeat, pulse, sweating, menstrual flow, the gluiness of sperm, the squatting position at urinating, the movements of the intestines, together with the sublime needs of the spirit, and our duality will find its form in it, without renouncing one zone or the other.

One More Day

Comprehension of good and evil is given in the running of the
    blood.
In a child's nestling close to its mother, she is security and
    warmth,
In night fears when we are small, in dread of the beast's fangs
    and in the terror of dark rooms,
In youthful infatuations where childhood delight finds comple-
    tion.

And should we discredit the idea for its modest origins?
Or should we say plainly that good is on the side of the living
And evil on the side of a doom that lurks to devour us?
Yes, good is an ally of being and the mirror of evil is nothing,
Good is brightness, evil darkness, good high, evil low,
According to the nature of our bodies, of our language.

The same can be said of beauty. It should not exist.
There is not only no reason for it, but an argument against.
Yet undoubtedly it is, and is different from ugliness.

The voices of birds outside the window when they greet the
    morning
And iridescent stripes of light blazing on the floor,
Or the horizon with a wavy line where the peach-colored sky
    and the dark-blue mountains meet.
Or the architecture of a tree, the slimness of a column crowned
    with green.

All that, hasn't it been invoked for centuries
As a mystery which, in one instant, will be suddenly revealed?
And the old artist thinks that all his life he has only trained his
hand.
One more day and he will enter the core as one enters a flower.

And though the good is weak, beauty is very strong.
Nonbeing sprawls, everywhere it turns into ash whole expanses
of being,
It masquerades in shapes and colors that imitate existence
And no one would know it, if they did not know that it was
ugly.

And when people cease to believe that there is good and evil
Only beauty will call to them and save them
So that they still know how to say: this is true and that is false.

Winter

The pungent smells of a California winter,
Grayness and rosiness, an almost transparent full moon.
I add logs to the fire, I drink and I ponder.

"In Ilawa," the news item said, "at age 70
Died Aleksander Rymkiewicz, poet."

He was the youngest in our group. I patronized him slightly,
Just as I patronized others for their inferior minds
Though they had many virtues I couldn't touch.

And so I am here, approaching the end
Of the century and of my life. Proud of my strength
Yet embarrassed by the clearness of the view.

Avant-gardes mixed with blood.
The ashes of inconceivable arts.
An omnium-gatherum of chaos.

I passed judgment on that. Though marked myself.
This hasn't been the age for the righteous and the decent.
I know what it means to beget monsters
And to recognize in them myself.

You, moon, You, Aleksander, fire of cedar logs.
Waters close over us, a name lasts but an instant.
Not important whether the generations hold us in memory.
Great was that chase with the hounds for the unattainable meaning
    of the world.

[*36*

And now I am ready to keep running
When the sun rises beyond the borderlands of death.
I already see mountain ridges in the heavenly forest
Where, beyond every essence, a new essence waits.

You, music of my late years, I am called
By a sound and a color which are more and more perfect.

Do not die out, fire. Enter my dreams, love.
Be young forever, seasons of the earth.

From the beginning writing was for me a means of redeeming my true or imaginary worthlessness. Perhaps initially it was accompanied by some romantic hope of acquiring an everlasting name. But in reality it was mainly the desire to win merit through edifying literature. Alas, without much success, for I was hampered by the distance between what I felt myself to be and what I would have appeared to my readers.

Of course literature should be edifying. Whoever, because of an exceptionally avid imagination, succumbed to the bad influence of books, cannot think otherwise. The word "edifying" is pronounced sarcastically today and that is sufficient proof that something is wrong with us. What great works of literature were not edifying? Homer perhaps? Or *The Divine Comedy?* Or *Don Quixote?* Or *Leaves of Grass?*

I was liberating myself and that was bitter. Having been eminently susceptible to words, to all propaganda. Then from year to year the language of chronicles, lectures, speeches, poems, tragedies, novels grew thinner and thinner, till it took on the consistency of smoke, completely different from that of the tangible though incomprehensible reality.

Perhaps one thing only is of great concern to me: whether I come closer, slowly, by detours, circling here and there, moving away, returning, but always with one aim. Coming closer

[*38*

to what? To a knowledge, though of what kind I do not know, to comprehension.

Fear of my early youth: that I grow up, i.e., that I lose intensity in pursuing things of the mind. But I am past seventy and I have been living guided by incessant curiosity, passion, striving.

Had I not granted recognition to myself, I could not have survived so long without the recognition of my fellow men, besides a chosen few. Thence a moral lesson, that things we are ashamed of are sometimes useful.

The language of literature in the twentieth century has been steeped in unbelief. Making use of that language, I was able to show only a small bit of my believing temperament. For we had crossed a certain borderline separating us from another literature, somewhat old-fashioned, deserving respect but artistically inferior.

You were the servant of time and you were right. No one can jump out of his skin. Yet a season arrives, perhaps the one you were waiting for, when you say, "I am a contemporary of Aristotle and St. Augustine and St. Thomas Aquinas, why should I care about the opinions of those who live now or will live after us?" Anyway the same measure applies both to centuries near and distant.

[*39*

Where does humility come from? From sitting down and putting little signs on paper with the hope of expressing something. I am able to spend whole days on the occupation, but as soon as I finish I see that I did not express anything. I would like to consider myself a genius; I do not manage it. To tell the truth, I don't know where the geniuses of literature are whom I should envy. Those of the past are caught in the manners and style of their period; those of today move with difficulty in a transparent jam that is slowly coagulating. And I, always insatiable, just as in this moment when I come to the window, see a tower with a clock, snow underneath it on the lawns of the Ann Arbor campus, a girl walking on a pathway, and the very act of being here, by the window, in this moment similar to any other, i.e., unrepeatable, with the whiteness of the snow and the movement of legs observed from above, is sufficient to initiate my lament on the insufficiency of language.

Sparkles from the Wheel

Where the city's ceaseless crowd moves on the livelong day,
Withdrawn I join a group of children watching, I pause aside
    with them.

By the curb toward the edge of the flagging,
A knife-grinder works at his wheel sharpening a great knife,
Bending over he carefully holds it to the stone, by foot and
    knee,
With measur'd tread he turns rapidly, as he presses with light
    but firm hand,
Forth issue then in copious golden jets,
Sparkles from the wheel.

The scene and all its belongings, how they seize and affect me,
The sad sharp-chinn'd old man with worn clothes and broad
    shoulder-band of leather,
Myself effusing and fluid, a phantom curiously floating, now
    here absorb'd and arrested,
The group, (an unminded point set in a vast surrounding)
The attentive, quiet children, the loud, proud, restive base of
    the streets,
The low hoarse purr of the whirling stone, the light-press'd
    blade,
Diffusing, dropping, sideways-darting, in tiny showers of gold,
Sparkles from the wheel.

—WALT WHITMAN

[41

Miracles

Why, who makes much of a miracle?
As to me I know of nothing else but miracles,
Whether I walk the streets of Manhattan,
Or dart my sight over the roofs of houses toward the sky,
Or wade with naked feet along the beach just in the edge of the
    water,
Or stand under trees in the woods,
Or talk by day with anyone I love, or sleep in the bed at night
    with anyone I love,
Or sit at table at dinner with the rest.

Or look at strangers opposite me riding in the car,
Or watch honeybees busy around the hive of a summer fore-
    noon,
Or animals feeding in the fields,
Or birds, or the wonderfulness of insects in the air,
Or the wonderfulness of the sundown, or of stars shining so
    quiet and bright,
Or the exquisite delicate thin curve of the new moon in spring;
These with the rest, one and all, are to me miracles,
The whole referring, yet each distinct and in its place.

To me every hour of the light and dark is a miracle,
Every cubic inch of space is a miracle,
Every square yard of the surface of the earth is spread with the
    same,
Every foot of the interior swarms with the same.
To me the sea is a continual miracle,

The fishes that swim—the rocks—the motion of the waves—
    the ships with men in them,
What stranger miracles are there?

—WALT WHITMAN

Cavalry Crossing a Ford

A line in long array where they wind betwixt green islands,
They take a serpentine course, their arms flash in the sun—hark
    to the musical clank,
Behold the brown-faced men, each group, each person a pic-
    ture, the negligent rest on the saddles,
Some emerge on the opposite bank, others are just entering the
    ford—while,
Scarlet and blue and snowy white,
The guidon flags flutter gayly in the wind.

—WALT WHITMAN

Bivouac on a Mountain Side

I see before me now a traveling army halting,
Below a fertile valley spread, with barns and the orchards of
    summer,
Behind, the terraced sides of a mountain, abrupt, in places ris-
    ing high,
Broken, with rocks, with clinging cedars, with tall shapes din-
    gily seen,
The numerous campfires scattered near and far, some away up
    on the mountain,

The shadowy forms of men and horses, looming, large-sized,
    flickering,
And over all the sky—the sky! far, far out of reach, studded,
    breaking out, the eternal stars.

—WALT WHITMAN

To a Locomotive in Winter

Thee for my recitative,
Thee in the driving storm even as now, the snow, the winter-
day declining,
Thee in thy panoply, thy measur'd dual throbbing and thy beat
convulsive,
Thy black cylindric body, golden brass and silvery steel,
Thy ponderous side-bars, parallel and connecting rods, gyrat-
ing, shuttling at thy sides,
Thy metrical, now swelling pant and roar, now tapering in the
distance,
Thy great protruding headlight fix'd in front,
Thy long, pale, floating vapor-pennants, tinged with delicate
purple,
The dense and murky clouds out-belching from thy smoke-
stack,
Thy knitted frame, thy springs and valves, the tremulous twin-
kle of thy wheels,
Thy train of cars, behind obedient, merrily following,
Through gale or calm, now swift, now slack, yet steadily
careering;
Type of the modern—emblem of motion and power—pulse of
the continent,
For once come serve the Muse and merge in verse, even as here
I see thee,
With storm and buffeting gusts of wind and falling snow,
By day thy warning ringing bell to sound its notes,
By night thy silent signal lamps to swing.

Fierce-throated beauty!
Roll through my chant with all thy lawless music, thy swinging
    lamps at night,
Thy madly-whistled laughter, echoing, rumbling like an earth-
    quake, rousing all,
Law of thyself complete, thine own track firmly holding,
(No sweetness debonair of tearful harp or glib piano thine),
Thy trills of shrieks by rock and hills return'd,
Launched o'er the prairies wide, across the lakes,
To the free skies unpent and glad and strong.

—WALT WHITMAN

Part Three

Unattainable Earth

The whole round Earth resides in my consciousness, which means that I live in a time when the successive attempts to found a universal State, beginning with Alexander the Great, can at last find support in imagination.

A dark spruce forest, where people used to say there were still bears, announces Kiejdzie whose mistress does not allow anybody to hunt in her domain. Every time I passed by there, I felt the lure of mystery. But I was never to learn what the manor of Kiejdzie was like or she herself, what everyday life in it was like, what she became.

A Boy

Standing on a boulder you cast a line,
Your bare feet rounded by the flickering water
Of your native river thick with water lilies.
And who are you, staring at the float
While you listen to echoes, the clatter of paddles?
What is the stigma you received, young master,
You who are ill with your apartness
And have one longing: to be just like the others?
I know your story and I learned your future.
Dressed as a gypsy girl I could stop by the river
And tell your fortune: fame and a lot of money,
Without knowledge, though, of the price to be paid
Which one does not admit to the envious.
One thing is certain: in you, there are two natures.
The miserly, the prudent one against the generous.
For many years you will attempt to reconcile them
Till all your works have grown small
And you will prize only uncalculated gifts,
Greatheartedness, self-forgetful giving,
Without monuments, books, and human memory.

In my dream I was traveling, probably by car, through a hilly countryside, little valleys where everyday life is lived, a so-so one, and a voice reproached me for squandering my time on trifles, instead of writing about the essence of life, which is so-so-ness.

Probably all my voyages in dreams have a model in one, very real, by cart from Raudonka on the Wilno-Jaszuny road for a kermess in Turgiele. A sandy road with ruts, always either up or down, stubble fields on hills in the sun, here and there a spruce grove, then alders by streams, huts, well-sweeps.

In Salem

Now you must bear with your poor soul.
Guilt only, where you proudly stood.
Diplomas, honors, parchment scrolls,
Lectures at Harvard, doctor's hood:
Tongues in which nothing loudly calls.

I walk somewhere at the world's end,
In Wilno, by a bridge called Green.
An old woman reads postcards I send
From Baton Rouge or Oberlin.
We both have reasons to lament.

Dreams visit me year after year,
They are expendable, J. W.
What might have been is just thin air,
A loss we long ago outgrew.
So why do we talk and why do we care?

You know that tangible things escape
The art of words and tricks of mind.
Early I guessed what was my fate,
The sentence was already signed
At Haven Street and the Outgate.

In Salem, by a spinning wheel
I felt I, too, lived yesterday,
My river Lethe is the Wilia,
Forest bonfires like censers sway,
So many names and all unreal.

Translated by the author

[54

1913

I betook myself to Italy right after the harvest.
That year 1913 the McCormick harvester
For the first time moved across our fields
Leaving behind stubble altogether unlike that
Left by the sickle or the scythe of the reapers.
On the same train, but in third class,
My factotum Yosel rode to his kin in Grodno.
I had my supper there, in the refreshment room,
At a long table under rubber plants.
I recollected the high bridge over the Niemen
As the train wound out of an Alpine pass.
And I woke up by the waters, grayish blue
In the radiance of the pearly lagoon,
In the city where a traveler forgets who he is.
By the waters of Lethe I saw the future.
Is this my century? Another continent,
With Yosel's grandson we sit together
Talking of our poet friends. Incarnated,
Young again, yet identical with my older self.
What strange costumes, how strange the street is,
And I myself unable to speak of what I know.
No lesson for the living can be drawn from it.
I closed my eyes and my face felt the sun,
Here, now, drinking coffee in Piazza San Marco.

Photos from Krasnogruda just received, taken a couple of months ago. The autumnal park, the reeds of the lake. In each I recognize clearly the spot from which the photographer shot them. What would we say about a man of the last century, reminiscing in 1884 about his youth in 1830? That the two epochs were completely different, that he would have been old and his memory fuzzy. But it is not so. The sensual perception of every detail is as sharp as when I was nineteen and I have the same feeling, as if I were rowing again toward the alders on the headland or walking uphill in the direction of the veranda, glimpsed among the trees, a feeling of being here only for a moment. In Krasnogruda? On earth? Though that district of rocks and lakes with an overcast sky never seemed to me like home. As to the era, the dry leaves visible in the photograph are more important, and since all the people who once walked there are dead by now, the persistence of soils, plants, seasons imprints itself even more strongly, and so does the transitoriness of human affairs. Even in that great division between our land of the living and their densely populated land of shadows, eras, fashions, mores lose their meaning completely, as if to let us imagine that the dead of all places and all centuries, made equal, communicate with each other.

At Dawn

How enduring, how we need durability.
The sky before sunrise is soaked with light.
Rosy color tints buildings, bridges, and the Seine.
I was here when she, with whom I walk, wasn't born yet
And the cities on a distant plain stood intact
Before they rose in the air with the dust of sepulchral brick
And the people who lived there didn't know.
Only this moment at dawn is real to me.
The bygone lives are like my own past life, uncertain.
I cast a spell on the city asking it to last.

At Noon

At a mountain inn, high above the bulky green of chestnuts,
The three of us were sitting next to an Italian family
Under the tiered levels of pine forests.
Nearby a little girl pumped water from a well.
The air was huge with the voice of swallows.
Ooo, I heard a singing in me, ooo.
What a noon, no other like it will recur,
Now when I am sitting next to her and her
While the stages of past life come together
And a jug of wine stands on a checkered tablecloth.
The granite rocks of that island were washed by the sea.
The three of us were one self-delighting thought
And the resinous scent of Corsican summer was with us.

Return to Cracow in 1880

So I returned here from the big capitals,
To a town in a narrow valley under the cathedral hill
With royal tombs. To a square under the tower
And the shrill trumpet sounding noon, breaking
Its note in half because the Tartar arrow
Has once again struck the trumpeter.
And pigeons. And the garish kerchiefs of women selling flowers.
And groups chattering under the Gothic portico of the church.
My trunk of books arrived, this time for good.
What I know of my laborious life: it was lived.
Faces are paler in memory than on daguerreotypes.
I don't need to write memos and letters every morning.
Others will take over, always with the same hope,
The one we know is senseless and devote our lives to.
My country will remain what it is, the backyard of empires,
Nursing its humiliation with provincial daydreams.
I leave for a morning walk tapping with my cane:
The places of old people are taken by new old people
And where the girls once strolled in their rustling skirts,
New ones are strolling, proud of their beauty.
And children trundle hoops for more than half a century.
In a basement a cobbler looks up from his bench,
A hunchback passes by with his inner lament,
Then a fashionable lady, a fat image of the deadly sins.
So the Earth endures, in every petty matter
And in the lives of men, irreversible.
And it seems a relief. To win? To lose?
What for, if the world will forget us anyway.

[59

The City

The city exulted, all in flowers.
Soon it will end: a fashion, a phase, the epoch, life.
The terror and sweetness of a final dissolution.
Let the first bombs fall without delay.

Preparation

Still one more year of preparation.
Tomorrow at the latest I'll start working on a great book
In which my century will appear as it really was.
The sun will rise over the righteous and the wicked.
Springs and autumns will unerringly return,
In a wet thicket a thrush will build his nest lined with clay
And foxes will learn their foxy natures.

And that will be the subject, with addenda. Thus: armies
Running across frozen plains, shouting a curse
In a many-voiced chorus; the cannon of a tank
Growing immense at the corner of a street; the ride at dusk
Into a camp with watchtowers and barbed wire.

No, it won't happen tomorrow. In five or ten years.
I still think too much about the mothers
And ask what is man born of woman.
He curls himself up and protects his head
While he is kicked by heavy boots; on fire and running,
He burns with bright flame; a bulldozer sweeps him into a clay
    pit.
Her child. Embracing a teddy bear. Conceived in ecstasy.

I haven't learned yet to speak as I should, calmly.

World and Justice

"Rabbi Levi said:
If it is the world you seek, there can be no justice;
and if it is justice you seek, there can be no world.
Why do you grasp the rope by both ends,
seeking both the world and justice?
Let one of them go,
for if you do not relent a little, the world cannot endure."

—*Hammer on the Rock, A Short Midrash Reader,*
edited by Nahum Glatzer, 1962.

How do we live on the surface pretending not to feel the terror?
In this epoch which I have experienced and which has not been
narrated? In this and not any other destiny, my own, of which
I think at night, unable to tell verdict from chance. How can
we be so restrained, conversing in cautious words?

"Si Dieu aura pitié de cette planète—je me demande parfois s'il peut y avoir des raisons divines d'en avoir pitié. Malgré tous les rapprochements qu'on fait avec des époques passées, il me semble qu'il y a dans celle-ci quelque chose de sans précédent: l'énorme diffusion, surtout grâce aux media, d'une arrogance stupide.

C'est comme une décomposition, simultanée et conjuguée, de la pensée et de la volonté."★

—From a letter of Jeanne

"I could not have a better life than the one I had," she writes to me in February 1983 from Warsaw, Irena who has lived through the occupation of her country by two enemy armies, had to live in hiding trailed by the Gestapo, then adapt herself to life under Communist rule, witness the terror and the workers' responses in 1956, 1970, 1976, 1980, and the martial law proclaimed in December 1981.

★"Will God take pity on this planet—I ask myself sometimes whether there are any divine reasons to take pity on it. In spite of parallels drawn between past epochs and our own, I believe there is in this one something without precedent: a massive diffusion, first of all thanks to the media, of stupid arrogance. It is like a decomposition, simultaneous and conjoint, of thought and will."

[63

Who will assure me that I perceive the world the same way other people do? It is not improbable that I am a deviation from a norm, an oddity, a mutation, and that I have no access to what they experience. And if that is the case, what right do I have to pronounce general opinions on man, history, the difference between good and evil, society, systems; as if I did not guess that my difference, though hidden, influences my judgments, changes proportions?

What is the core of twentieth-century experience? Undoubtedly the impotence of the individual. Everything around us moves, becomes, tends toward, occurs, while a particular man has practically no influence on it. How is it possible that what is created by people themselves is so little dependent on their wishes? Hardly a hundred years ago man, endowed with reason and will, expected a state of things in which obstacles would disappear, especially those which hamper the full unveiling of his reason and will.

What about people like Solzhenitsyn or Walesa? Isn't their role in the twentieth century more considerable than that of an average-sized state?—asks a friend of mine.

INSCRIPT

"Yet what is perpetually present, what it is therefore permissible to love, is the very possibility of misfortune. The three facets of our being are always exposed to it. Our flesh is fragile; any piece of matter in motion can pierce it, tear it, smash it, or derange forever one of our internal mechanisms. Our soul is vulnerable, subject to depressions without cause, pitiably dependent on all manner of things and beings which are in their turn fragile and capricious. Our social self on which the feeling of our existence practically depends is always and entirely exposed to every possible hazard. The center of our being is bound to those three things with fibers so tender that it feels their wounds, to the point of bleeding. What diminishes or destroys our social prestige, especially our right to consideration, seems to alter or abolish our very essence, so much so that illusion is our very substance."

—SIMONE WEIL,
L'amour de Dieu et le malheur

I don't like the Western way of thinking. I could say: the way Western intellectuals think, but then I would pass over the transformation that has occurred during the last few decades. And the transformation (not a sudden one, though suddenly present, like pubescence or senility) consists in the disappearance of a distinction between the enlightened—the knowledgeable, the progressive, the mentally liberated—and the so-called masses. That great schism has ended and we are returned to a unified world view, as was the case in the Middle Ages when a theologian, a cooper and a field hand believed the same things. Schools, television and newspapers have allied themselves to turn minds in the direction desired by the liberal intelligentsia, and so the victory came: an image of the world which is in force for all of us, under a penalty equivalent to the ancient penalties of pillory and stake: that is, ridicule.

With not-quite truth
and not-quite art
and not-quite law
and not-quite science

Under not-quite heaven
on the not-quite earth
the not-quite guiltless
and the not-quite degraded

Poland. Why only the lowest? Why only the highest, and nothing in between? And why does loyalty to Polishness only harm it, while rebellion against it covers it with splendor?

The ivy-like character of the Polish language. As opposed to the self-sufficient vigor of Russian close to its folk roots. Ivy and vines should not necessarily be considered inferior, but they must have something to entwine, and that is why the rhythm of Latin was so important for those who wrote in Polish.

I owe much to my high school, a good school of the years of independence (1918–1939), but probably I am most grateful to it for seven years of Latin. And to the Roman Catholic church for the Latin of its Sunday mass.

The difficulty of tuning the voice. Or, to put it differently, the difficulty of tracing a borderline in the sentence, which in Polish tends to spill capriciously into asides or melt into garrulity. The lack of the sense of form in old Polish authors is disquieting, even in those from the Golden Age.

Can the lack of a sense of form, noticeable in the language, in literature, be the cause of a given country's downfall? Not the lack of a sense of form as a consequence of the downfall, that would be too simple, but the other way around. Only then does the question sound venomous enough.

Communism has given Polish literature an incredible chance. Always historically oriented, but preoccupied only with Poland's history, suddenly it was confronted with a universal theme. Few writers drew the appropriate conclusions.

Mythologies of the unlucky conquered nations.

Part Four

Consciousness

Consciousness

1. Consciousness enclosed in itself every separate birch
And the woods of New Hampshire, covered in May with green
    haze.
The faces of people are in it without number, the courses
Of planets, and things past and a portent of the future.
Then one should extract from it what one can, slowly,
Not trusting anybody. And it won't be much, for language is
    weak.

2. It is alien and useless to the hot lands of the living.
Leaves renew themselves, birds celebrate their nuptials
Without its help. And a couple on the bank of a river
Feel their bodies draw close right now, possessed by a nameless
    power.

3. I think that I am here, on this earth,
To present a report on it, but to whom I don't know.
As if I were sent so that whatever takes place
Has meaning because it changes into memory.

4. Fat and lean, old and young, male and female,
Carrying bags and valises, they defile in the corridors of an air-
    port.
And suddenly I feel it is impossible.
It is the reverse side of a Gobelin
And behind there is the other which explains everything.

5. Now, not any time, here, in America
I try to isolate what matters to me most.
I neither absolve nor condemn myself.

The torments of a boy who wanted to be nice
And spent a number of years at the project.

The shame of whispering to the confessional grille
Behind which heavy breath and a hot ear.

The monstrance undressed from its patterned robe,
A little sun rimmed with sculptured rays.

Evening devotions of the household in May,
Litanies to the Maiden,
Mother of the Creator.

And I, conscience, contain the orchestra of regimental brasses
On which the moustachioed ones blew for the Elevation.

And musket volleys on Easter Saturday night
When the cold dawn had hardly reddened.

I am fond of sumptuous garments and disguises
Even if there is no truth in the painted Jesus.

Sometimes believing, sometimes not believing,
With others like myself I unite in worship.

Into the labyrinth of gilded baroque cornices
I penetrate, called by the saints of the Lord.

I make my pilgrimage to the miraculous places
Where a spring spurted suddenly from rock.

[74

I enter the common childishness and brittleness
Of the sons and daughters of the human tribe.

And I preserve faithfully the prayer in the cathedral:
Jesus Christ, son of God, enlighten me, a sinner.

6. I—consciousness—originate in skin,
Smooth or covered with thickets of hair.
The stubby cheek, the pubes, and the groin
Are mine exclusively, though not only mine.
And at the same instant, he or she—consciousness—
Examines its body in a mirror,
Recognizing a familiar which is not quite its own.

Do I, when I touch one flesh in the mirror,
Touch every flesh, learn consciousness of the other?

Or perhaps not at all, and it, unattainable,
Perceives in its own, strictly its own, manner?

7. You will never know what I feel, she said,
Because you are filling me and are not filled.

8. The warmth of dogs and the essence, inscrutable, of dog-
    gishness.
Yet I feel it. In the lolling of the humid tongue,
In the melancholy velvet of the eyes,
In the scent of fur, different from our own, yet related.
Our humanness becomes more marked then,
The common one, pulsating, slavering, hairy,

[75

Though for the dogs it is we who are like gods
Disappearing in crystal palaces of reason,
Busy with activities beyond comprehension.

I want to believe that the forces above us,
Engaged in doings we cannot imitate,
Touch our cheeks and our hair sometimes
And feel in themselves this poor flesh and blood.

9. Every ritual, astonishing human arrangements.
The dresses in which they move, more durable than they are,
The gestures that freeze in air, to be filled by those born later,
Words that were pronounced by the dead, here and still in use.
And erotic: they guess under the fabric
Dark triangles of hair, are attentive to convexities in silk.
Faithful to the ritual because it differs so much from their natures,
And soars above them, above the warmth of mucous mem-
    brane,
On the incomprehensible borderline between mind and flesh.

10. Certainly, I did not reveal what I really thought.
Why should I reveal it? To multiply misunderstandings?
And reveal to whom? They are born, they mature
In a long pause and refuse to know what comes later.
Anyway I won't avert anything. All my life it was like that:
To know and not be able to avert. I must give them reason.
They have no use for lives lived sometime in the future
And the torments of their descendants are not their concern.

[76

What use are you? In your writings there is nothing except immense amazement.

In an intermediary phase, after the end of one era and before the beginning of a new one. Such as I am, with habits and beliefs acquired in childhood, which were impossible to maintain, to which I was loyal and disloyal, self-contradictory, a voyager through the lands of dream, legend, myth, I would not like to pretend I reason clearly.

INSCRIPT

"Whatever one knows, he knows for himself only and he should keep it secret. As soon as he reveals it, contradictions appear, and if he begins to argue, he will lose his equilibrium, while what is best in him will be, if not annihilated, at least shaken."

— GOETHE, *Wilhelm Meister*

It is not true that what we think about our world now in the twentieth century can be reduced to reflections on the eternal human condition. Men have never lived in such conditions before; they have not been besieged by questions like ours. While respecting tradition and recognizing analogies, we must remember that we are trying to name a new experience.

There is only one theme: an era is coming to an end which lasted nearly two thousand years, when religion had primacy of place in relation to philosophy, science and art; no doubt this simply meant that people believed in Heaven and Hell. These disappeared from imagination and no poet or painter would be able to populate them again, though the models of Hell exist here on earth.

Man never had a clear representation of life after death. But now, when priests and the faithful say the words "life eternal," no representations appear at all.

"Denying, believing, and doubting completely are to man what running is to a horse."

—PASCAL, *Pensées*

The gates of darkness expend so much energy trying to eradi-cate divine things that one may see in it a providential revenge of history. Who could bring himself otherwise to confirm so actively the greatest longing of man?

On Prayer

You ask me how to pray to someone who is not.
All I know is that prayer constructs a velvet bridge
And walking it we are aloft, as on a springboard,
Above landscapes the color of ripe gold
Transformed by a magic stopping of the sun.
That bridge leads to the shore of Reversal
Where everything is just the opposite and the word *is*
Unveils a meaning we hardly envisioned.
Notice: I say *we;* there, every one, separately,
Feels compassion for others entangled in the flesh
And knows that if there is no other shore
They will walk that aerial bridge all the same.

"To wait for faith in order to be able to pray is to put the cart before the horse. Our way leads from the physical to the spiritual."

—O. MILOSZ

My late friend Father J. S. did not believe in God. But he believed God, the revelation of God, and he always stressed the difference.

Had the tortures, the concentration camps and gas chambers, been something from outside, a disturbance of the normal order of things. But what about the breast of a twenty-six-year-old woman riddled with cancer, a sudden heart attack, the slow dying of the mentally defective? Oppression only confirms what we know already about the fate of all living matter. So why do we read that God created man in his image and likeness? It means, no more nor less, that God has a human face, that there is in Him a human Logos, Adam Kadmon. There is no way out of this contradiction. Except perhaps believing in the Fall and in an unlimited human capacity to return to that divine humanity.

"For me the principal proof of the existence of God is the joy I experience any time I think that God is."

—RENÉ LE SENNE, *La découverte de Dieu*

"If, as a consistent atheist, one replaces God [taken as a consciousness and will surpassing human consciousness and will] with Society [the State] and History, one must say that whatever is outside the range of social and historical verification is forever relegated to the domain of opinion [*doxa*]." Thus the great promoter of Hegel in France, Alexandre Kojève [Kozhevnikov]. And this one sentence suffices as a prediction of the epoch when man, deprived of the notion of truth, will succumb to total dependence on the State.

In Orwell's *1984* the inquisitor O'Brien asks Winston whether in his opinion the past really exists.

"You are no metaphysician, Winston," he said. "Until this moment you had never considered what is meant by existence. I will put it more precisely. Does the past exist concretely, in space? Is there somewhere or other a place, a world of solid objects, where the past is still happening?"

"No."

"Then where does the past exist, if at all?"

"In records. It is written down."

"In records. And—?"

"In the mind. In human memories."

"In memory. Very well, then. We, the Party, control all records and we control all memories. Then we control the past, do we not?"

How to deny it? Any reality exists for us only to the extent that it is seen and by the same token submitted to the operations of the mind. Whatever surrounds us reaches us already transformed by concepts, i.e., by language, spoken, written or pictorial. This applies even more to past things, which are accessible only through a double transformation, the one made once by the mind and the one made again at the moment of recollection. The past does not exist in any other guise. Whoever maintains the contrary simply asserts that the unembraceable kaleidoscope of time is present every quarter of a second in a super-mind which sees past, present and future simultaneously. In other words, he believes in God. Such seems to be the foundation of objective truth, searched for by the agnostic Orwell.

[*83*

A famous fragment of St. Augustine's *Confessions* on time:

"So what is time? If no one asks me, I know; if I want to explain it to a person who asks, I do not know anymore and yet I affirm with certainty that, had nothing passed, there would not be past time; had nothing existed, there would not be future time."

This probably means that time is not independent of the existence of things, it is not an element in which things subject to movement move. Not, to use another metaphor, a line conceived as extending infinitely back and forward. Where there are no things, time does not exist. And space exists only where there are things. Much later, in the age of Newton, people began to believe that time and space were containers inside of which matter moves. In this way they avoided thinking about Nothing, where there is no matter, no time, no space.

INSCRIPT

"It is not up to man to place the inevitable in time and space. The inevitable is somehow outside time and space. Materially unfulfilled, it exists in the shape of the present as well as of the past and the future in one divine instant."

—O. MILOSZ

INSCRIPT

"The two problems of love and death, inexhaustible sources of suffering, are indissolubly linked to the question of space. Man has only one desire: to live and to love eternally. Yet in space, as he represents it to himself, i.e., preexisting and containing him, everything has a beginning and an end. Created free, man has materialized his secret being and, together with it, Nature in the universal sense of the word. His madness prompted him to *situate* the containing space to which he ascribed a real existence; this space, in his sacrilegious thought, became stretched to infinity and identified with the spiritual absolute. Hell is precisely this. . . ."

—O. MILOSZ

Part Five

I, He, She

A young man of unspeakable ugliness was sitting in a barber's chair. His face, long, pale, sheeplike, was covered with bleeding pimples. The scissors were cutting gobbets of his yellow hair. I felt such disgust that the thought of finding myself soon in the same armchair and of submitting myself to the same scissors was unbearable to me. In this way I caught myself once more in my repugnance for the majority of the human tribe and, underneath that, was my attraction to the species opposed to them, the species of the good-looking, among whom, obviously, I counted myself.

Some are born humanized. Or so it seems to me when I think of all the anonymous saints and heroes of this century. Others have to humanize themselves slowly, and it sometimes takes dozens of years. It is hardly my fault if, trying to approach that goal in a lofty fashion, I ended up in falsities and self-delusions. Captive of my sensual nature, only through lovemaking was I able to experience myself dissolving in communion, alive among the living. A triumph of "I" (was it not?) allowed me to break out of the enclosure of my "I."

Do I love God? Or her? Or myself? I don't know how to differentiate and that makes me ashamed, as it is not only hard to confess but even to think. My piety is perhaps just the gratitude of serene flesh for breathing, for the rhythm of blood, for everything.

Father Ch., Many Years Later

Father Chomski, the vicar of Vaidotai parish,
Died at the age of ninety-seven, worrying till the end
About his parishioners, for no one would succeed him.

On the shore of the Pacific, I, his former pupil,
Was translating the Apocalypse from Greek into Polish,
Finding it the proper season for that labor.

They had to hold up his hands on both sides
When he raised the host and the wine above the altar.

He had been beaten by thugs of the Empire
Because he refused to bow before the world.

And I? Didn't I bow? The Great Spirit of Nonbeing,
The Prince of this World, has his own devices.

I did not want to serve him. I always labored
In order to at least delay his victory.

So that God might be resplendent with his angelic crowd,
He who is all-powerful but whose mill grinds slow.

He who in the huge war is defeated every day
And does not give signs through his churches.

To whom in our school chapel I vowed faithfulness
While Father Chomski approached on tiptoe and put out can-
    dles.

And yet I could not distinguish Him from the rhythm of my
     blood
And felt false reaching beyond it in my prayer.

I was not a spiritual man but flesh-enraptured,
Called to celebrate Dionysian dances.

And disobedient, curious, on the first step to Hell,
Easily enticed by the newest idea.

Hearing all around me: it is good to experience,
It is good to feel, be bold, free yourself from guilt.

Wanting to absorb everything, comprehend everything,
And darkness proved to be forebearing toward me.

Did I toil then against the world
Or, without knowing, was I with it and its own?

Helping the Ruler to tread with his iron boot
An earth that did not merit any better?

                  .   .   .

And yet it wasn't so, oh my accomplice in sin,
Eve under the apple tree, in the delightful garden.

I loved your breasts and your belly and your lips.
How to comprehend your otherness and sameness?

[*91*

Convex and concave, how do they complement each other?
How is it that we feel and think alike?

Our eyes seeing the same, our ears hearing the same,
Our touch making and unmaking the same world.

Not one, divided in two, not two, united in one:
The second I, so that I may be conscious of myself.

And together with you eat fruits from the Tree of Knowledge
And by twisting roads make our way through deserts.

                    .   .   .

By twisting roads from which one sees, below, the golden domes
of rising and sinking cities, mirages of undulating streets, hunt-
ers pursuing gazelles, a pastoral scene by a stream, plows at
noon resting in the fertile fields, so much and in such various-
ness, with a music in the air of pipes and flutes, with voices
calling, voices that once were. Twisting roads, uncounted centuries, but could I renounce what I received, consciousness,
knowledge, a never-fulfilled striving toward the aim? Even if it
was fated that the aim, of which for a long time nothing was
known, would hold our expectations up to ridicule. To renounce,
to close, and to mortify sight, hearing and touch, to break free
that way and not have to fear anymore that something will be
taken away from us—no, I did not know how to do that.

                    .   .   .

I sit down now and write in my defense.
The witnesses are old things, undimmed, dense

With the life of human hands: the intense reds
In stained glass, stone lacework, marble heads,

The dark gold calligraphies of magic, traces
Of red in alchemical script, marmoreal laces,

Maps on which the lands of faery glimmer,
Globes wrapped in black velvet and a shimmer

Of stars, the slow spokes of a millwheel
By a waterfall, lute songs, a bell's peal.

There I had my home, my refuge, my Exodus
From the Egypt of cosmic unreachableness.

.   .   .

All I have is the dexterity of my hands. I was *homo faber,* origi-
nator, maker, fabricator, builder. The sky above me was too
big, its numberless stars deprived me of my singularity. And
the line of time infinitely retreating and infinitely extending
annihilated each moment of my life. But when I hit a log in its
very center with an ax and saw suddenly the white of the split
wood, when I carved close-grained pear wood with a chisel, or
painted *Ledum palustre* or *Graphalium uliginosum* on soft thick
paper that held the color, or boiled elixirs according to an old
recipe, then the Dragon of the Universe, the great Egypt of
inexorable galactic rotations, had no power over me, because I
was guided and protected by Eros, and whatever I was doing
grew immense and stood in front of me, here, right now.

[*93*

. . .

And thus, willy nilly, you sang my song?
And gave me everything beautiful and strong?

What comes from nothing and return to it? This:
Strength, exultation, abundance and bliss.

You danced a blind dance on the edge of a pit.
Blood gave you the rhythm. You chose to submit,

No truth in all that. It's nothing but fever.
The earth is mine forever and ever.

. . .

That voice, persecuting me, to be honest, every day.

I am unable to imagine myself among the disciples of Jesus
When they wandered through Asia Minor from city to city
And their words were preparing the Empire's collapse.

I was in the marketplace between amphoras of wine,
Under the arcade where tasty flitches of meat sizzled on a spit.
The dancers danced, the wrestlers gleamed with oil.
I was choosing among bright fabrics sold by merchants from
    overseas.

Who will refuse to pay homage to the statues of Caesar
If by his grace we are granted a reprieve?

[94

"Consequently, the whole of Creation is FEMALE and the love of the Lord for Himself in Creation is the love of *Man* for *Woman,* and the return to God is Conjunction or Marriage . . . (Creation is also the Church). . ."

—Note (in English) by O. Milosz in the margin
of Swedenborg's *The True Christian Religion*

INSCRIPT

"Humility. Woman *saves* man, for being *Love of Wisdom* she spares him the dangerous course of loving his own wisdom. That is the basis of *Conjugial Love.*"

—Note (in French) by O. Milosz in the margin
of Swedenborg's *Conjugial Love*

INSCRIPT

"They are made of amorous dough. As soon as they turn twelve, love has begun to take them somewhere. They see its glowing torch from afar and follow it through the half-light of childhood. . ."

—CARLO GOZZI, *Memorie inutile*

Initiation

Vanity and gluttony were always her sins
And I fell in love with her in the phase of life
When our scornful reason is the judge of others.

Then I went through a sudden initiation.
Not only did our skins like each other, tenderly,
And our genitals fit once and for all,
But her sleep at arm's length exerted its power
And her childhood in a city she visited dreaming.

Whatever was naive and shy in her
Or fearful in the disguise of self-assurance
Moved me, so that—we were so alike—
In an instant, not judging anymore,
I saw two sins of mine: vanity, gluttony.

Elegy for Y.Z.

Never forget that you are a son of the King.

—MARTIN BUBER

A year after your death, dear Y.Z.,
I flew from Houston to San Francisco
And remembered our meeting on Third Avenue
When we took such a liking to each other.
You told me then that as a child you had never seen a forest,
Only a brick wall outside a window,
And I felt sorry for you because
So much disinheritance is our portion.
If you were the king's daughter, you didn't know it.
No fatherland with a castle at the meeting of two rivers,
No procession in June in the blue smoke of incense.
You were humble and did not ask questions.
You shrugged: who after all am I
To walk in splendor wearing a myrtle wreath?
Fleshly, woundable, pitiable, ironic,
You went with men casually, out of unconcern,
And smoked as if you were courting cancer.
I knew your dream: to have a home
With curtains and a flower to be watered in the morning.
That dream was to come true, to no avail.
And our past moment: the mating of birds
Without intent, reflection, nearly airborne
Over the splendor of autumn dogwoods and maples;
Even in our memory it left hardly a trace.
I am grateful, for I learned something from you,
Though I haven't been able to capture it in words:
On this earth, where there is no palm and no scepter,
Under a sky that rolls up like a tent,

[98

Some compassion for us people, some goodness
And, simply, tenderness, dear Y.Z.

P.S. Really I am more concerned than words would indicate.
I perform a pitiful rite for all of us.
I would like everyone to know they are the king's children
And to be sure of their immortal souls,
I.e., to believe that what is most their own is imperishable
And persists like the things they touch,
Now seen by me beyond time's border:
Her comb, her tube of cream and her lipstick
On an extramundane table.

Anka

In what hat, from what epoch,
Is Anka posing in the photograph,
Above her brow the wing of a killed bird?
Now she is one of them, beyond the threshold
Where there are no men, no women,
And the prophet does not give separate sermons
To the ones covered with shawls
So that their long hair does not provoke lust,
And to the tanned, bearded men in draped burnouses.
Saved from the furnaces of World War II,
Trying on dresses in reflected mirrors
And blouses and necklaces and rings.
With a hairstyle and makeup for the wars of her career,
Happy to go to bed or just talk over wine,
The owner of a beautiful apartment, full of sculpture.
Left to herself till the end of the world,
How does she manage now, fleshless?
And what could the prophet find to say, when he has no thought
Of the hair under a shawl and the secret
Fragrance of skin and of ointments?

The worst possible sexual education: a taboo imposed by the Catholic church plus romantic literature elevating love to unreal heights plus the obscene language of my peers. After all, I was nearly born in the nineteenth century, and I have no tender feelings for it.

And yes, everything was coming to pass on the brink. The brink of destruction by fire, water, starvation, the invasion of Germans, of Saracens, of Turks, by typhoid, plague, fever, cancer, heart attack, stroke, yes, on the very brink, in the one moment when we felt that the beautiful architecture of our bodies was exposed to the onslaught of death.

Tendresse. I prefer this word to its Polish equivalent. When one feels a lump in one's throat because the creature at whom one looks is so frail, vulnerable, so mortal, then *tendresse.*

To wake up in the morning and try to reconstruct our dream, in order to allay the suspicion that the dream said more about us than we want to confess.

We always hope that somehow everything will be all right, because others are better than we are.

The cruelty of a look. I glanced at her without seeing her, or saw her only as part of the space surrounding me, and she felt I had looked at her as at a thing.

What does salvation mean, what does damnation mean? In a line at the post office, I look at people and am repulsed by their ugliness. Ugly women, ugly men, like gathered millennia of hairy and bowlegged tribes. And perhaps someone else feels otherwise. Deep in every man is hidden a grain determining his attitude toward his fellow man, perhaps his love or lack of love. I don't know either my kind of grain or that of others. Perhaps we should really concede that we are, in advance, before our birth, predestined for salvation or damnation?

Prayers of men. Perhaps they should ask, most of all, to be spared that one short moment when what they suspected about themselves, not willing to confess it, is revealed.

You Felons on Trial in Courts

You felons on trial in courts,
You convicts in prison cells, you sentenced assassins chain'd
and handcuff'd with iron,
Who am I too that I am not on trial or in prison?
Me ruthless and devilish as any, that my wrists are not chain'd
with iron, or my ankles with iron?
You prostitutes flaunting over the trottoirs or obscene in your
rooms,
Who am I that I should call you more obscene than myself?
O culpable! I acknowledge—I expose!
(O admirers, praise not me—compliment not me—you make
me wince,
I see what you do not—I know what you do not.)

Inside these breastbones I lie smutch'd and choked,
Beneath this face that appears so impassive hell's tides contin-
ually run.
Lusts and wickedness are acceptable to me,
I walk with delinquents with passionate love,
I feel I am of them—I belong to those convicts and prostitutes
myself,
And henceforth I will not deny them—for how can I deny myself?

—WALT WHITMAN

[103

We Two, How Long We Were Fool'd

We two, how long we were fool'd,
Now transmuted, we swiftly escape as Nature escapes,
We are Nature, long have we been absent, but now we return.
We become plants, trunks, foliage, roots, bark,
We are bedded in the ground, we are rocks,
We are oaks, we grow in the openings side by side,
We browse, we are two among the wild herds spontaneous as
    any,
We are two fishes swimming in the sea together,
We are what locust blossoms are, we drop scent around lanes
    mornings and evenings,
We are also the coarse smut of beasts, vegetables, minerals,
We are two predatory hawks, we soar above and look down,
We are two resplendent suns, we it is who balance ourselves
    orbic and stellar, we are as two comets,
We prowl fang'd and four-footed in the woods, we spring on
    prey,
We are two clouds forenoons and afternoons driving overhead,
We are seas mingling, we are two of those cheerful waves roll-
    ing over each other and interwetting each other,
We are what the atmosphere is, transparent, receptive, per-
    vious, impervious,
We are snow, rain, cold, darkness, we are each product and
    influence of the globe,
We have circled and circled till we have arrived home again, we
    two,
We have voided all but freedom and all but our own joy.

—WALT WHITMAN

Once I Pass'd Through a Populous City

Once I pass'd through a populous city imprinting my brain for
    future use with its shows, architecture, customs, tradi-
    tions,
Yet now of all that city I remember only a woman I casually
    met there who detain'd me for love of me,
Day by day and night by night we were together—all else has
    long been forgotten by me,
I remember I say only that woman who passionately clung to
    me,
Again we wander, we love, we separate again,
Again she holds me by the hand, I must not go,
I see her close beside me with silent lips sad and tremulous.

—WALT WHITMAN

O Living Always, Always Dying

O living always, always dying!
O the burials of me past and present,
O me while I stride ahead, material, visible, imperious as ever;
O me, what I was for years, now dead (I lament not, I am
content);
O to disengage myself from those corpses of me, which I turn
and look at where I cast them,
To pass on (O living! always living!) and leave the corpses behind.

—WALT WHITMAN

[106

What Am I After All

What am I after all but a child, pleas'd with the sound of my
    own name? repeating it over and over;
I stand apart to hear—it never tires me.

To you your name also;
Did you think there was nothing but two or three pronuncia-
    tions in the sound of your name?

—WALT WHITMAN

Hast Never Come to Thee an Hour

Hast never come to thee an hour,
A sudden gleam divine, precipitating, bursting all these bub-
    bles, fashions, wealth?
These eager business aims—books, politics, art, amours,
To utter nothingness?

—WALT WHITMAN

The Last Invocation

At the last, tenderly,
From the walls of the powerful fortress'd house,
From the clasp of the knitted locks, from the keep of the well-
    closed doors,
Let me be wafted.

Let me glide noiselessly forth;
With the key of softness unlock the locks—with a whisper,
Set ope the doors O soul.

Tenderly—be not impatient,
(Strong is your hold O mortal flesh,
Strong is your hold O love).

—WALT WHITMAN

I think of everyday life which somehow goes on in spite of invasions, sieges and upheavals. Also of those who died in the time when every year became a date in a history book. Not like Halaburda, deported to a gulag and dying there of dysentery, or Gasiulis executed by the invaders for tearing down their posters. No, I think of others, of Miss Anna and Miss Dora, for instance, old, ill, lonely. And yet there must have been a neighbor near them in their last moments, one of those eternal old women-samaritans, who straightened the pillow, gave them a sip of water, and closed their eyelids.

The notion of sin, abandoned to keep pace with progress, was needed and useful. For I, a sinner, bore a burden and was able to throw it down, it was not myself. Now my guilt is placed inside, it is my genes, my fate, my nature. And yet I know from experience that I am like the water of a river, reflecting the changeable colors of the banks it flows between, storms, clouds, the blue of the sky, colorless itself.

Resurrection. All tangible things—material things, as people used to say—change into light and their shape is preserved in it. After the end of our time, in a meta-time, they return as light condensed, though not condensed into the previous state of matter. By virtue of incomprehensible force, they are then essences alone. The essence of every human being, without all that accrued to it, without age, illness, makeup, disguises, pretending.

[*110*

My clear realization that men and women in church, gray hair, bald pates, tight little curls, are not themselves but a form acquired during their lives among their fellow beings, that in reality they are just children and deserve to have the artificial colors of the social theater washed from them, and also the years they lived, so that there remains in them a true shape of the human species, childhood, youth, readiness, exploration.

The church. The only place where people are neither turned toward other people nor are they only spectators (as they are in a theater). A man with his face turned toward other people is never free from defensive reflexes, i.e., the meeting of eyes is a duel of two subjects. A man confronted with *sacrum* does not need to defend himself. The position of the priest with his back to the faithful, as the leader of a chorus, made sense.

A view of the old, pale, mumbling, leaning on their canes, neither men nor women, since the difference of sex has disappeared. And nearby broad-shouldered boys and doe-eyed girls lightly strutting, obviously the same, only a few years earlier. It looks as if an anonymous current passed through people, and then abandoned their shells in a few turns of the hourglass, leaving behind, instead of live creatures, an assortment of broken dolls. How, looking at it, to believe in the vocation of one unique soul?

[*111*

The bay at dawn the color of melted tin and on it, far away, a moving boat with one minuscule man, standing, keeping before him the long line of a rudder. He and the civilization of fifty-story buildings, galactic vehicles, electronic music. Who is he? Is he its part? So tiny, forever unfathomed, all by himself, or no more than a punctuation mark?

The torture of dying for weeks, months, sometimes years. It is waiting for the majority of us. And nothing? And we accept such an order of things? But how can one accept monstrosity?

A decent man cannot believe that a good God wanted such a world.

Theodicy

No, it won't do, my sweet theologians.
Desire will not save the morality of God.
If he created beings able to choose between good and evil,
And they chose, and the world lies in iniquity,
Nevertheless, there is pain, and the undeserved torture of crea-
    tures
Which would find its explanation only by assuming
The existence of an archetypal Paradise
And a pre-human downfall so grave
That the world of matter received its shape from diabolic power.

"Whence comes evil? people ask. Many theodicies, very little different from each other, give answers to this question—answers which satisfy only their authors (do they satisfy them?) and the lovers of amusing literature. As for the others, theodicies annoy them, and this annoyance is directly proportional to the intensity with which the question of evil pursues an individual. When this question acquires for us the importance that it had, for example, for Job, every theodicy appears sacrilegious. Every attempt to "explain" his misfortunes does nothing but aggravate them in the eyes of Job. . . . To put the matter otherwise, one can ask (sometimes, as in the case of Job, the question is inevitable), 'Whence comes evil?', but one cannot answer this question. And it is only when the philosophers recognize that this question and many other questions should not be answered, that they will know that one does not always ask to obtain answers are, that there are questions whose significance lies precisely in their not admitting answers, because answers kill them.

Is this not quite understandable? What is to be done? Be patient. Man must resign himself to many things which are still more difficult."

—LEV SHESTOV, *Athens and Jerusalem*

From Joseph Czapski's letter of March 4, 1983:

My dear Czeslaw,

I indulge in debauchery and instead of my work which clamors, I write to you. Your letter in which you say how much you miss Father Sadzik—believe me, I also miss him cruelly though I didn't have the close relationship with him that you did. You end your letter with one sentence that hits the core—of what? Of the subject tormenting man and imposing itself on him: *Providence.* Anything one thinks and says of it is enveloped in words of *consolation* which only veil Truth, and the truth can only be accepted transcendentally, on another plane. I cannot believe that God will save Poland because the Holy Virgin of Czestochowa celebrates her 600th anniversary, I'm sorry. When I came back from Russia, Marynia said that God, Providence, protected me because I had something to say, to accomplish. I felt then that the Truth had been physically insulted. How many hundreds of people I knew, how many millions whom I was aware of, were perishing from starvation and cold, and all of them "had something to say," all of them had mothers, wives, lovers who lived in an agony of longing and waiting. You ask whether Providence extends to *history!* The truth most difficult to accept (S. Weil) is that the world is ruled *only by chance,* that God has no power over it, i.e., his power, his help is of another dimension. Providence, yes, but it exists only when it sends both happiness and misfortune and a man *really* living in God receives the blows and the happiness *in the same manner* as he receives Grace. We are far below that dimension; *nevertheless we know it exists.*

The mechanical character of crimes, wrongs, downfalls of Poland, of its greatness and pettiness and of that truly noble-minded *young wave* [illegible] now trampled upon, should we call all that Providence too? Providence because for the time being we do not murder but are murdered! I am going to tell you a story, an old one. Before 1939 somebody told me (I listened to it as a fable, perhaps partly true but it stayed in my memory somehow) that after Rome had been taken by the barbarians, a crowd of Romans fled to Africa, where St. Augustine was still alive. With sorrow, with bitterness, they asked *why* God inflicts calamities on Rome, of all places, because at that time it was already Christian.

St. Augustine called in a young monk, Orosius. "I am already old and I'm not strong, but you should write a history of the world so that it will teach people that catastrophes and calamities have been in history *always.*" I have remembered Orosius ever since, even though I didn't try to verify the truthfulness of the story. Then, in an old, huge encyclopedia which I bought in Rome during the war, I found that everything happened *precisely that way:* Orosius wrote the book after St. Augustine's death and its subject was a demonstration that calamities were and would be *always.*

Rescue by Providence?

That *light* we can find at the very bottom of abandonment and misfortune. What Providence can save our world which is sinking and which will probably be reborn with *new hopes somewhere else?*

Lately a friend of mine was on Cyprus for four days and he tells me that one walks there on thousands of fragments of mosaics. Those are fragments of mosaic floors from more than two thousand years ago. In some places little bridges have been constructed to protect the remains of them. *"Et maintenant il n'*

[*116*

y a rien." *That* island also implored Providence. Every one of us, leaving this life, preserves from his past, from memories, from quotations by which he lived, no more than a few words that he salvages from a receding memory.

Cas de contredictoires vrais: Dieu existe, Dieu n'existe pas. Je suis tout à fait sûre qu' il y un Dieu, en ce sens que je suis tout à fait sûre que mon amour n'est pas illusion. Je suis tout à fait sûre qu'il n'y a pas de Dieu, en ce sens que je suis tout à fait sûre que rien de réel ne ressemble à ce que je peux concevoir quand je prononce ce nom. Mais cela que je ne peux concevoir n'est pas une illusion. ⋆ *—S. Weil*

Empty Cyprus with its remnants of innumerable mosaic floors, Poland trampled upon, coldly violated, hit at what was best in her—the apocalypse which has already begun—since always!

I did not want to write you a letter full of bathos, but only by looking "with open eyes at the inhuman earth" can one breathe with a feeling that one does not *lie,* and then, in rare, brief moments, help comes.

P.S. Please do not be surprised that in a letter written for you and about you, I feed upon quotations. I find in them *an answer*

⋆ *The case of true contradictions: God exists, God does not exist. I am absolutely sure that there is a God, in the sense that I am absolutely sure my love is not an illusion. I am absolutely sure that there is no God, in the sense that I am absolutely sure nothing real resembles what I can conceive when I pronounce that name. And yet something I cannot conceive is not an illusion.*

[*117*

such as I wouldn't be able to find myself, so now I live on quotations and they rescue me.

Lorsque on ne s'efforce pas d' exprimer l' inexprimable, alors rien ne se perd et l' inexprimable *est contenu* inexprimablement *dans ce qui est exprimé.* ★—*L. Wittgenstein*

We do *not* know: perhaps it must be so, we do not know anything about the value of that which we give—it is *inexprimablement contenu dans ce qui est exprimé.*

★ *When one does not force himself to express the inexpressible, nothing is lost and the inexpressible is contained inexpressibly in that which is expressed.*

The miracle according to Simone Weil: not a violation of laws but accordance with laws unknown to us. Thinking along the same lines I can believe that the Holy Virgin appeared at Fatima and Lourdes, but it is much more difficult to believe in God's rule over this world.

The twentieth century, the century of moralizing. How dare you assure yourself that your existence has a meaning inscribed in the book of all things, inaccessible to the human mind, and that you are under special protection! What about others? Their prayers have not been answered, but it is of no concern to you, skunk (salaud). This is the central thought of the twentieth-century philosopher, Sartre the moralist.

The sense of justice is an enemy of prayer. How to ask for a miracle if innumerable human beings, just like yourself, begged and it was refused to them? Very well, but is it really worthwhile to force oneself to be so just? To pretend to be superhuman? An angel?

Interior memory preserves everything we have experienced and thought during our whole life, not even one second is lacking. Yet we have no access to it except in moments as short as the twinkling of an eye. The belief that, with death, man perishes forever implies that the oversensitive tape is recorded for nobody. This seems to me improbable, but any time I think that somebody may read it, the image of Judgment immediately imposes itself.

[*119*

Since she lacks faith and because of that may find herself in Hell, could I, having such tenderness for her, leave her there alone? Were I to do that, I would deserve Hell, all right.

We do not know the Hells and Heavens of people we pass in the street. There are two possible perspectives. According to the first, on a minuscule ball of earth, in a smudge of mold called a city, some microorganisms move around, less durable than mayflies. And the internal states of beings, deprived of any reason for their existence, perfectly interchangeable, what importance can they have? According to the second perspective, that of a reversed telescope, every one of these beings grows up to the size of a cathedral and surpasses in its complexity any nature, living or inert. Only in the second case can we see that no two persons are identical and that we may at best try to guess what is going on inside our fellow men.

It is possible, perhaps it is even easiest, to represent people as an animal species ruled by a limited number of reflexes that can be named and catalogued. Then the so–called mature mind triumphs and falsity disappears, the kind proper to poetry which elevates man and his affairs to another dimension simply because it has recourse to language, i.e., form. All poetry becomes then a childish occupation, deserving no more than condescension from a mature mind.

[*120*

INSCRIPT

"Every strong and pure being feels he is something else than merely man and refuses, naively fearing it, to recognize himself one of an infinite number of copies of the species or of a type which repeats itself."

—PAUL VALÉRY, *Variétés*

Self-contentment. Lack of self-contentment. Image of myself in the mirror, with a physical potency, a mental potency. Image of myself in my own eyes as a good, perhaps noble creature, well disposed toward my fellow men. Or just the opposite. Both attitudes seem to me beneath the concern of a truly wise man. I have never been one. But at least I respect and admire people who know how to think the least possible about themselves, either well or ill.

One more image of myself: calm, detached from others' as well as my own judgments on my person, taking things as they come, serenely, settled in my center, in my true "I" of which Zen Buddhism speaks. And is it not one more subterfuge of the ego? Perhaps not for others, but for me it is one more entanglement, like the purity of the soul, in childhood, after confession, the day we receive Communion, when we feel light and happy with our well-cleansed interior.

Do you know what the gravest sins in your life are?—I have made too many mistakes to trust my ability not to err now when thinking of my past.

I am not what I am. My essence escapes me. Here A does not equal A. It is a durable achievement of existential philosophy to remind us that we should not think of our past as definitely settled, for we are not a stone or a tree. In other words, my past changes every minute according to the meaning given it now, in this moment.

Jeanne, a disciple of Karl Jaspers, taught me the philosophy of freedom, which consists in being aware that a choice made now, today, projects itself backward and changes our past actions. That was the period of my harsh struggle against *delectatio morosa* to which I have always been prone. Monks suffering from *delectatio morosa* would plunge into meditation on their sins and found it a good way to shirk their daily tasks. The philosophy of freedom, practiced by existentialists, took over the classical methods of confessors and spiritual guides, precisely in that it advises us to direct our sight always ahead, not backwards. Largely thanks to its counsels, I stopped meditating and set about my work, which has always been to me an escape forward.

Soloviev's Parable

Two hermits were saving their souls in the desert of Nitria. Their caves were not very far apart, but they never talked to each other and would only announce their presence by singing psalms. In this manner they spent many years and their fame spread through Egypt and neighboring countries. It happened once that the devil succeeded in putting into their souls, both at the same time, the same intent, and without a word to each other they packed up their work—baskets and mats made of palm leaves and twigs—and went off to Alexandria. There they sold their goods and then caroused with drunkards and harlots for three days and nights, after which they went back to their desert. One of them grieved, weeping bitterly:—Now I am lost entirely, cursed man that I am! No prayers can amend such rage and depravity. All my fasting and night vigils and prayers wasted, at one stroke I destroyed everything forever!

The other walked with him and sang psalms in a cheerful voice.

—Are you out of your mind, or what?

—Why do you ask?

—So you do not grieve at all?

—Why should I grieve?

—What! After Alexandria?

—What about Alexandria? Glory to the Highest who protects that pious and illustrious city!

—But we, what were we doing in Alexandria?

—You know what we were doing: we were selling our baskets, we worshiped at Saint Mark's, visited other churches, called on the pious governor of the city, conversed with the prioress Leonilla who is so kind to monks . . .

—But didn't we spend our nights in a brothel?

—God forbid! We spent our evenings at the patriarch's court.

—Holy martyrs! He is insane. And where did we soak ourselves in wine?

—We tasted wine and healthful foods at the patriarch's table on the occasion of the Presentation of the Most Holy Virgin.

—Miserable! And whom were we kissing, not to mention worse things?

—We were honored on our departure with a holy kiss from the father of fathers, the most blessed archbishop of the great city of Alexandria and of the whole of Egypt, Libya and Pentapolis, Cyrus-Timotheus.

—Are you laughing in my face? Or after the abominations of yesterday has the devil taken hold of you? Whores kissed you, you accursed fool!

—Well, I don't know who the devil took hold of: me, who rejoices in the gifts of God and in the kindness shown to us by God's servants, or you who are raving and calling the house of our blessed father and shepherd a brothel, insulting him and his God-loving clergy by calling them whores.

—You, miserable heretic! Offspring of Arius! Bloody lips of loathsome Apolinarius!

And the hermit who grieved over his downfall threw himself on his comrade and began to beat him with all his might. After that, they walked in silence to their caves. All night long the repentant one tormented himself, filled the desert with groans and laments, tore his hair, threw himself on the ground, dashing his head against it, while the other quietly and joyfully sang psalms. In the morning the repentant one was struck by a thought: since, by exertions of many years, I have won special blessings of the Holy Spirit, which had already begun to reveal themselves in signs and miracles, now, *because of that,* I have, by giving myself to the abominations of the flesh, committed a sin against the Holy Spirit and that sin is, according to the word of God, unpardonable in this age and in future ages. But if I am irrevocably doomed, what am I doing here in the desert? And he went to Alexandria and gave himself to a life of debauchery.

One day, when he was in need of money, he, together with some other idlers, robbed and murdered a wealthy merchant. The crime was discovered, he was tried by the city court, and, sentenced to death, he died without repentance. During the same time his comrade, continuing his life of self-denial, attained a high degree of saintliness and acquired fame by his great miracles, so that one word of his was enough to cause women who had been sterile for many years to conceive and give birth to children of the male sex. When the day of his death arrived, his withered and emaciated body, as if blooming with beauty and youth, became radiant and filled the air with fragrance. After his death a monastery was built upon his miraculous relics and his name passed from the church of Alexandria to Byzantium, wherefrom it found its way to the church calendars of Kiev and Moscow.

—*Three Conversations*

Part Six

A Table

Table I

Only this table is certain. Heavy. Of massive wood.
At which we are feasting as others have before us,
Sensing under the varnish the touch of other fingers.
Everything else is doubtful. We too, appearing
For a moment in the guise of men or women
(Why either-or?), in preordained dress.
I stare at her, as if for the first time.
And at him. And at her. So that I can recall them
In what unearthly latitude or kingdom?
Preparing myself for what moment?
For what departure from among the ashes?
If I am here, entire, if I am cutting meat
In this tavern by the wobbly splendor of the sea.

Table II

In a tavern by the wobbly splendor of the sea,
I move as in an aquarium, aware of disappearing,
For we are all so mortal that we hardly live.
I am pleased by this union, even if funereal,
Of sights, gestures, touches, now and in ages past.
I believed my entreaties would bring time to a standstill.
I learned compliance, as others did before me.
And I only examine what endures here:
The knives with horn handles, the tin basins,
Blue porcelain, strong though brittle,
And, like a rock embattled in the flow
And polished to a gloss, this table of heavy wood.

INSCRIPT

"There is communion between soul and soul. The souls of the gods are in communion with those of men, and the souls of men with those of creatures without reason."

—*Corpus Hermeticum*

INSCRIPT

"There are two gifts which God has bestowed on man alone, and on no other mortal creature. These two are mind and speech; and the gift of speech is equivalent to immortality. If a man uses these two gifts rightly, he will differ in nothing from the immortals; or rather, he will differ from them only in this, that he is embodied upon earth; and when he quits his body, mind and speech will be his guides, and by them he will be brought in to the troops of gods and the souls that have attained to bliss."

—*Corpus Hermeticum*

The incessant striving of the mind to embrace the world in the infinite variety of its forms with the help of science or art is, like the pursuit of any object of desire, erotic. Eros moves both physicists and poets. If, as Swedenborg and Blake affirm, death does not interrupt that striving and Heaven is full of the incessant activity of inventive minds, Eros outlasts both life and death.

What did I think in the city of Kyoto? I thought that I joined my hands in prayer, made a bow, and lit an incense stick. I thought that I had lived long ago, lived now, and would live once again, beyond the endless cycle of deaths and births.

In Kyoto I was happy, that is, the past was blurred and the future without plan or desire. Not unlike a day in July for a boy who wakes up early, listens to the whistle of an oriole, and is on the run all day long, till dusk. I reflected on the odd gift of forgetting. For I could not, after all, get rid of remembering things I did not want to remember and sometimes it seemed to me that I was maneuvering to do so, like those new generations for whom the unpleasant truth about our century has been superseded by dates in a history book.

O life. O entering an enchanted garden where everything is touch and vision. It seemed to me that night that a gate closed behind me and that I would stay in the garden forever, and in a more real one than those I have known before.

[*132*

My-ness

"My parents, my husband, my brother, my sister."
I am listening in a cafeteria at breakfast.
The women's voices rustle, fulfill themselves
In a ritual no doubt necessary.
I glance sidelong at their moving lips
And I delight in being here on earth
For one more moment, with them, here on earth,
To celebrate our tiny, tiny my-ness.

INSCRIPT

"Before I began studying Zen, I saw mountains as mountains, rivers as rivers. When I learned some Zen, mountains ceased to be mountains, rivers to be rivers. But now, when I have understood Zen, I am in accord with myself and again I see mountains as mountains, rivers as rivers."

—SAISHO

Thankfulness

You gave me gifts, God-Enchanter.
I give you thanks for good and ill.
Eternal light in everything on earth.
As now, so on the day after my death.

INSCRIPT

"When we have two explanations of something, caution advises us to keep the simpler one for ourselves; for the least clear explanation is, at times, more persuasive to an uninitiated mind, i.e., a mind still naively fond of so-called profound thoughts."

—O. MILOSZ

How could I have expected that after a long life I would understand no more than to wake up at night and to repeat: strange, strange, strange, o how strange, how strange. O how funny and strange.

This is the life I always wanted to have. Civic concerns exclusively outside, and inside a contemplation of being itself, an occupation sufficient to fill twenty-four hours. And where I was, on what continent, in what city, made no difference.

Yes, this is a plenitude I searched for. Found not in books of philosophy, or on church benches, or in flagellating myself with discipline. After a day of varied activities, to feel at dawn my oneness with remembered people, despite a thought about my person separated from others.

[*136*

Nature soon bores me, I lose my taste for it, since boredom and nausea are nearly the same. Had I found myself on a desert island, I would have multiplied gods, favorable or ill-disposed, of the forces and the powers, and would have associated only with them.

After all, Nature was not the object of my contemplation. It was human society in the great cities of the modern era, "the pleasures of the depraved animal," as Baudelaire says. Animality in disguise, masks, rouge, mascara, the pre-copulatory rites, feasts of trailing dresses whirling in a street dance. Ravished by the incomparable mockery of fashion, surrendering to it, as if undergoing a transformation into somebody else behind the scenes in a theater. I was unable to fathom that element, I was unable to embrace and comprehend it, and to think meant to move in it, observing at the same time and from a distance myself and others.

The life of civilization was for me like a dream from which I tried to wake up in vain. Or—and this is also true—my life was such a dream.

Hans Post, his Brazilian landscapes painted around 1650. As in all Dutch landscape painters, what moves me is a contrast between the earth and a group of people dead long ago, in this case Brazilian Indians who disappeared both as particular beings and as a tribe. Solidarity with the tiny figures in whom our hopes and our troubles persisted for a while and can be looked at through a magnifying glass.

How does a good boy behave, if he has received the gift of a peculiar vision that denudes and annihilates human mores, so that he must remain all his life *outside?* He dodges, he pretends, invents ways to appear the same as others.

Love of life, passion for life. Perhaps one feels it also in one's youth, but differently and with different words. One must liberate oneself, at least to some extent, from complexities, from taking one's fate too much to heart, before being able to rejoice simply because one is alive among the living.

Poet at Seventy

Thus, brother theologian, here you are,
Connoisseur of heavens and abysses,
Year after year perfecting your art,
Choosing bookish wisdom for your mistress,
Only to discover you wander in the dark.

Ai, humiliated to the bone
By tricks that crafty reason plays,
You searched for peace in human homes
But they, like sailboats, glide away,
Their goal and port, alas, unknown.

You sit in taverns drinking wine,
Pleased by the hubbub and the din,
Voices grow loud and then decline
As if played out by a machine
And you accept your quarantine.

On this sad earth no time to grieve,
Love potions every spring are brewing,
Your heart, in magic, finds relief,
Though Lenten dirges cut your cooing.
And thus you learn how to forgive.

Voracious, frivolous and dazed
As if your time were without end
You run around and loudly praise
Theatrum where the flesh pretends
To win the game of nights and days.

[*139*

In plumes and scales to fly and crawl,
Put on mascara, fluffy dresses,
Attempt to play like beast and fowl,
Forgetting interstellar spaces:
Try, my philosopher, this world.

And all your wisdom came to nothing
Though many years you worked and strived
With only one reward and trophy:
Your happiness to be alive
And sorrow that your life is closing.

—Translated by the author

To find my home in one sentence, concise, as if hammered in metal. Not to enchant anybody. Not to earn a lasting name in posterity. An unnamed need for order, for rhythm, for form, which three words are opposed to chaos and nothingness.